Be a Good Little Widow

A FUNERAL

by Bekah Brunstetter

A SAMUEL FRENCH ACTING EDITION

SAMUEL FRENCH

FOUNDED 1830

NEW YORK HOLLYWOOD LONDON TORONTO

SAMUELFRENCH.COM

ISBN 978-0-573-69969-6   Printed in U.S.A.   #28062

MUSIC USE NOTE

IMPORTANT BILLING AND CREDIT REQUIREMENTS

Commissioned and developed by Ars Nova
Jason Eagan, Artistic Director; Jeremy Blocker, Managing Director

World Premiere produced by Ars Nova
511 West 54th Street, New York
www.arsnovanyc.com

BE A GOOD LITTLE WIDOW was first produced by Ars Nova in New York City on May 2, 2011. The performance was directed by Stephen Brackett, with sets by Daniel Zimmerman, costumes by Jessica Pabst, lighting design by Burke Brown, and sound design by Bart Fasbender. The cast was as follows:

MELODY	Wrenn Schmidt
CRAIG	Chad Hoeppner
HOPE	Jill Eikenberry
BRAD	Jonny Orsini

CHARACTERS

MELODY – a young wife, 26

CRAIG – her slightly older husband, 30

BRAD – Craig's friend and co-worker; Melody's age

HOPE – mid-50s, Craig's mother, a widow since '82

MUSIC

Many ages and many kinds.

I.

(A nice living room. A couch, a coffee table, a TV.)

*(**MELODY** stands in front of the TV, fork in hand, zoning out.)*

CRAIG. *(voiceover of voicemail)* Hey Mel. I'm on my way home finally I'll be there in – seven to ten minutes – I don't know if you are getting this, you didn't pick up, it's – 7:43 so I'll be there by 8 the latest. Love you. Oh, it's Craig.

*(**CRAIG** enters, weary from a flight, in the crisp French blue of corporate America.)*

(He rolls a sad black suitcase.)

Hey!

MELODY. Hey!

*(She goes to **CRAIG**, kissing him.)*

How was your flight?

CRAIG. Long and stupid.

MELODY. Awwwwwwwwww

*(**CRAIG**'s already on his blackberry checking emails, engrossed in it.)*

CRAIG. Sorry – there's this – I just have to check this real fast –

MELODY. You hungry?

CRAIG. Big time.

MELODY. I got Thai!

CRAIG. Score.

MELODY. Pad Thai. Witthhhhhhhh tofu.

CRAIG. Ew.

MELODY. It's good for you!

CRAIG. Fine. What'd you do today?

MELODY. I did stuff today.

CRAIG. I know –

MELODY. There's nothing to do.

CRAIG. There are things to do in Connecticut.

MELODY. I checked out that yoga place!

CRAIG. Yeah was it good?

MELODY. Bunch of old ladies queefing.

(*pointing to it, it's hideous*)

And I found this lamp!!!

CRAIG. Where?

MELODY. Thrift store!

CRAIG. *Nice!*

MELODY. And I unpacked the last box! It was labeled books but it did not contain books!

CRAIG. Yeah what was in it?

MELODY. Ummm cables and extension cords –

Hold on this bitch is about to get punched –

(*Eyes on TV. Punch.*)

Nice!

I've seen this one like eight times.

Yeah cables and stuff and I didn't know what to do with it so I put it in the hall closet. Which is kind of like unpacking it.

CRAIG. Thanks for doing that.

MELODY. ALSO I organized my sweaters by color which made me really happy. Which is sad.

CRAIG. Do mine next?

MELODY. It'd take me two minutes. Blue; Gray.

CRAIG. Ahhhhhhhh It's good to be home.

MELODY. For a whole week! You spoil me.

CRAIG. Actually um –

They've got me going to Chicago Monday –

I'm sorry they just dropped it on me –

MELODY. You said you were going to start being gone LESS –

CRAIG. It'll be better after this merger I *promise.*

MELODY. But it's been MORE. You can't just freaking leave / me here

CRAIG. I know, I just – we just have to give it some time!

MELODY. That's what we've been doing!!

CRAIG. Are you pissed?

(beat)

MELODY. I know. It's not your fault.

(beat)

CRAIG. Hey c'mere!

MELODY. What?

*(**CRAIG** puts his arms around her. **MELODY** smiles.)*

CRAIG. I wanna a kiss.

MELODY. I kissed you!

CRAIG. No I want like a real kiss. Like a welcome home kiss.

*(**MELODY** gives him a kiss, a bit longer and deeper.)*

MELODY. Like that?

CRAIG. Yeah that's better –

MELODY. Better than what?

CRAIG. Nothing.

MELODY. What?

CRAIG. I like the big soft kisses not the / like

MELODY. *(hurt for some reason)* Well sometimes I kiss you and your mouth is all small and tight and it's kind of like I'm trying to make out with a butthole.

CRAIG. Big kiss –

(BIG KISS.)

(He then puts his arms around her, starts to slow dance with her. She's uncomfortable, he's loving it.)

MELODY. Ha what're you doing?

CRAIG. Dancing with my wife in my new house.

(They dance.)

Because I'm actually here for a minute and not in a stinky hotel room or on a plane squished next to some fat mathematician.

MELODY. Was he really that fat?

CRAIG. I don't wanna be a dick or anything but seriously the guy needed two seats.

(He tries to twirl her. It doesn't work.)

MELODY. If we're gonna do this we need music.

(She separates from him, mutes the TV, dashes to her iPod, pink and on a dock, and selects something like Louis Armstrong – "When We are Dancing, I get Ideas.*)

CRAIG. What's this?

MELODY. Louis Armstrong!

CRAIG. Ohhhhh yeah!

MELODY. I downloaded a bunch!

(She returns to him. They dance, a bit better.)

(But the moment is not nearly as romantic as the music, as it never can be.)

MELODY. I'm hungry.

CRAIG. Just another minute.

MELODY. This song makes me feel like I'm in love.

CRAIG. You're not?

MELODY. No I am, just like moreso.

(They dance.)

Music helps you access your emotions. If you're having trouble – accessing an emotion generally, a song will take you there.

CRAIG. You know what?

I think you'd be an awesome therapist.

---

*See Music Use Note on Page 3.

MELODY. Stop it –

CRAIG. What?

MELODY. You don't have to like suggest careers for me –

CRAIG. I know! I didn't say anything!

MELODY. I'm going to do something / I just don't know what for yet okay?

CRAIG. I was just saying

MELODY. I'm only three years outta college it's normal for a person to take some / time to

CRAIG. Maybe my Mom could help you get into real estate?

MELODY. Gross, no.

CRAIG. We gotta have her over for dinner soon or she's just gonna show up. With dinner.

MELODY. I just – want the place to be ready.

CRAIG. It looks great!

MELODY. Yeah?

CRAIG. She's gonna love it.

(He kisses her. Tries to start something.)

MELODY. Weird.

CRAIG. What?

MELODY. Don't talk about your mom then try and make out with me.

(Beat. They separate.)

Should we eat now, or –

CRAIG. Yeah! I gotta drop a load off first. Drop the kids off at the pool.

MELODY. I hate it when you say that.

CRAIG. You love it.

MELODY. Just use the spray.

CRAIG. I will.

(beat)

MELODY. Love you!

CRAIG. Love you.

(The music and its romance swell, but there they are, standing apart from each other, looking at each other like strangers.)

(Transition. **HOPE** *arrives for dinner. Stands with* **MELODY***, inspecting the room.)*

(An uncomfortable silence.)

HOPE. Is there – I thought there was a fireplace?

MELODY. No –

HOPE. I *love* my fireplace, it is HEAVEN. My fireplace and a good book and a nice glass of a Bordeaux.

MELODY. Yeah – no fireplace!

Great weather! We've been having.

HOPE. Yes! Except for all of the rain!

MELODY. Right! Yes! It's been raining!

HOPE. Craig loves the rain.

MELODY. Yeah, he does.

    (beat)

I like it! It like never rains in Colorado.

HOPE. Yes! It was very dry at the wedding. The air was quite dry.

MELODY. I got some rain boots, they're fun.

    (beat)

HOPE. *(getting an idea)* You know what?

My friend Naomi from jazzercise! She has a daughter your age. She does – I think she's dentist? Or works for a dentist?

I'm going to give her your phone number.

MELODY. Aw – that's really sweet / but

HOPE. You'll have lunch! You'll make friends!

MELODY. Okay!

    (CRAIG *enters from kitchen.)*

CRAIG. How was the drive?

HOPE. Terrible traffic on 84. I left a bit late, the League coat drive ran late –

CRAIG. *(to* **MELODY***)* Mom's huge in the Widow's League, super active –

MELODY. I remember!

HOPE. It's just something I do!

CRAIG. She's a total asset, they wouldn't EXIST without her.

HOPE. We received DOUBLE the coat donations this year. DOUBLE.

MELODY. That's great!

CRAIG. You shoulda taken 91, shave off 20 minutes!

HOPE. But 84 is much more scenic, God that view of the river I could just eat it for LUNCH! Remember when we used to take that drive to your grandmother's?

MELODY. I'm so excited to finally have you over Mom!

*(***HOPE*** grimaces at the word, as does* ***MELODY*** *a little bit.)*

CRAIG. It's true, she's been freaking out / getting the place ready for you to see!

MELODY. I haven't been freaking out –

HOPE. Awwww, you don't have to make a fuss over little old me!

MELODY. I just wanted it to look nice for you.

HOPE. Awwww. Isn't that – that's so sweet.

(Beat. ***MELODY*** *waits for* ***HOPE*** *to compliment her house, but she doesn't.)*

MELODY. Your home is *so* beautiful I just…you have such beautiful taste!

HOPE. Awww – thank you –

(Beat. ***HOPE*** *looks around the room.)*

It is *such* a lovely little house! It's smaller than I remember.

CRAIG. C'mon Mom it's not *that* small –

HOPE. *(a Hope joke)* Where will you fit the grandchildren?

MELODY. The hall closet!

*(***CRAIG*** *laughs,* ***HOPE*** *does not.)*

CRAIG. She's kidding.

HOPE. Well it's *very* cozy. Like a little fairy tale.

CRAIG. I think she did a fantastic job.

HOPE. Very eclectic. Like a movie set!

MELODY. What kind of movie?

HOPE. You know one where there's – things. In the house. Honey is your stomach still bothering you?

CRAIG. No it's better!

MELODY. What's wrong with / your stomach?

HOPE. You've got to keep an eye on him.

MELODY. I – I do –

HOPE. You might have a wheat allergy! So many people these days are allergic to wheat!

CRAIG. I'm fine, it was just a / little

HOPE. Well I'm going to talk to my allergist for you.

MELODY. Should I put some music on?

HOPE. If you'd like! I'm enjoying the quiet.

MELODY. Sometimes I can hear silence.

(**HOPE** *nods, trying to agree.*)

HOPE. Well I *loved* the band at your wedding! So romantic, the slow songs –

It was fortunate you found a band, so quickly!

It all happened so quickly!

(*beat*)

Craig called me and said you were engaged and I thought *April Fools!!!!*

CRAIG. It was April *second*, Mom –

HOPE. I'd only met you the one time! So. But I was very happy.

Very happy.

So nice to have you back where you belong.

CRAIG. I know, it's great!

HOPE. You know what I was remembering?!

CRAIG. Oh God, what –

HOPE. When we played *circus?*

CRAIG. Ahh c'mon – that's just mean!

HOPE. He was in the backyard in a tutu – *I am in a Circus – I am in a Circus –*

MELODY. Ah – haha –

CRAIG. She always remembers this, I don't remember this –

HOPE. I'll never forget it.

MELODY. I used to pretend like I was homeless!

(*Beat.*)

HOPE. So what's for dinner, it smells *delicious!*

MELODY. I roasted a chicken. There is also a salad.

HOPE. That sounds just gorgeous!! Do you like to cook?

MELODY. Yeah I love it, I kind of just throw stuff together though, I'm not so much into recipes, I usually just – but I love that cookbook you gave me for Christmas. I love that!

There's a Whole Foods down the – I love Whole Foods.

(*beat*)

(**MELODY** *sits back down on the couch.*)

See can you hear that?

CRAIG. What?

MELODY. Silence!

HOPE. I hear the dishwasher?

MELODY. We don't have a dishwasher.

HOPE. How can you not have a dishwasher?

MELODY. I'm the dishwasher!

I'm just usually broken!

(*Beat.* **HOPE** *puts a hand on* **CRAIG**'s *knee.*)

HOPE. What time's your flight tomorrow?

CRAIG. Ungodly, 6 AM.

HOPE. Craig! How do they expect you to function?! That's ridiculous!

CRAIG. I'm a pro!

MELODY. He is a pro he's got like a whole / system

CRAIG. Then the next day, Detroit.

HOPE. Oh heavens why?

MELODY. That's what I / said

HOPE. Then Chicago then back home to the wife for a whole week!

MELODY. He calls me 'The Wife.'

CRAIG. She likes it.

MELODY. I do!

HOPE. It's a big word to live up to!

MELODY. Yes it is!

HOPE. When you pack him tonight, make sure he has plenty of socks. My boy has sweaty feet!

MELODY. When I p –

HOPE. When you pack him. Tonight.

(beat)

MELODY. May I offer you some brie?

HOPE. No thank you, dear.

MELODY. Okay.

(beat)

Why not?

HOPE. Pardon?

CRAIG. Saving room for dinner, huh?

HOPE. Indigestion.

MELODY. You *love* brie. Craig said it was your favorite.

HOPE. That was very sweet of you! It just looks a little – under-ripe.

CRAIG. *(to* **MELODY***)* The, um. You're supposed to take it outta the fridge, a few hours before.

HOPE. At least three hours before.

MELODY. *(to* **CRAIG***)* Why didn't you tell me?

CRAIG. I thought you already did!

MELODY. Well I didn't, I wish you had told me –

HOPE. I'm just going to the little girl's room. Wash my hands.

I'll give you two a moment.

MELODY. We don't need a moment.

HOPE. But I do have to use the restroom.

MELODY. Right down the hall, first door on the left – there's plenty of everything!

HOPE. Thank you.

(**HOPE** *goes.*)

(**CRAIG** *watches* **MELODY**.)

CRAIG. …*What?*

MELODY. Oh my God.

CRAIG. What?

MELODY. These pillows suck – why did I get these pillows – When I PACK you?!

CRAIG. Why are you freaking out??

MELODY. Your mom hates me!!

CRAIG. She does not / *hate*

MELODY. Okay well she doesn't like me very much.

CRAIG. Yes she does!!

MELODY. She doesn't.

Which really isn't fair because SOME people think I am *awesome.*

CRAIG. I think you're awesome.

MELODY. You're required to, by law.

CRAIG. Nope, it's my choice.

MELODY. She'll like me. She just has to get to know me.

CRAIG. Just be yourself.

MELODY. What is that?

CRAIG. ….What?

MELODY. Tell me what to be, and I'll be that.

(**HOPE** *re-emerges, sniffing the air.*)

HOPE. Is something burning?

MELODY. Oh crap –

Excuse me –

(**MELODY** *beelines for the kitchen.*)

(**HOPE** *joins* **CRAIG** *on the couch.* **CRAIG** *puts his arm around her.*)

(*a crash from the kitchen*)

CRAIG. *(off)* You okay baby?

MELODY *(offstage)* Yeah I'm good! Sorry!

(**HOPE** *smiles.*)

CRAIG. …What?

HOPE. She *is* a baby.

CRAIG. *Stop.*

HOPE. I ran into Stephanie's mother –

CRAIG. Ahhh –

HOPE. She's still not seeing anyone.

I don't think she ever got over you.

(*beat*)

I still think about her sometimes. Stephanie.

CRAIG. Well I don't. So – don't.

(*beat*)

HOPE. Are you happy?

CRAIG. Very much.

HOPE. You sure?

(*beat*)

CRAIG. *Yes.*

HOPE. Then so am I.

(*lights*)

(**HOPE** *is gone.*)

(*In the dark, the sun comes up. Very early in the morning.*)

(**CRAIG**, *in suit, comes in with a suitcase, finishing a cup of coffee.*)

(**MELODY** *comes in sleepily.*)

(*He kisses her goodbye.*)

(**MELODY** *stands alone in the house.*)

(*Lights shift to day.*)

II.

(Still in sleep clothes, She's sitting next to one of the boxes, sifting through it listlessly.)

(She goes to her iPod and selects a country song in the style of Dixie Chick's "Cowboy Take Me Away"*)

(MELODY *starts to cry, but it is sort of childish and pouty and small.)*

(She gives up, goes to the couch. Sits. Reaches for her phone. Calls.)

MELODY. *(on phone)* Hey Dad! What are you doing?

Oh yeah? What kind? YUM. With pecans? *(She laughs.)* What's Mom doing?

This morning I invented 'pizza omelet!' Yeah and then it's rolled up like a 'breakfast calzone.'

(Tears come to her eyes.)

No, Craig's good, he's fine, I don't know, he's just never here

But I'm okay.

No, I'm not crying. I'm fine! I'm *fine.*

Go to work.

Love you. Bye.

(MELODY *exits upstairs to her room, we hear voice-mails.)*

CRAIG. *(singing).*

I LOVE YOU MELODY

OH YES I DO

WHEN I'M NOT WITH YOU

I'M BLUE

Hey. We haven't taken off, we're delayed like two hours now, I just wanna get back to you.

And I think I left my iPod at home, is it there? Also there's no wireless and I gotta get this proposal in so Brad's gonna come over and grab it off my desktop, okay?

---

* Please see Music Use Note on Page 3.

Love you. Oh, it's Craig.

(Sound: Beep.)

MELODY. Hey.

You don't have to say "I love you its Craig" anymore cause I know your voice. Okay? And you don't have to – I mean *thank you* for doing it but you don't have to update me every second, it's stressing me out, I know you'll get here when you get here, okay?

(Sound: Beep.)

CRAIG. I'm not trying to update you every second I'm sorry I just, I thought you'd want to know. So I was just telling you.

We're taking off now.

Bye.

(Lights shift to:)

*(**MELODY**, watching TV.)*

(She is doing yoga on the floor.)

(The TV screen goes out. She futzes with the cable box, turning it on and off.)

(The doorbell rings.)

*(**MELODY** lets in **BRAD**, younger and hotter than Craig. Dark, slightly brooding, delicious. Craig's paralegal. He wears workout clothes.)*

(There is subtle tension between them, of the sexy variety. Chemistry, clearly.)

MELODY. Hey Brad.

BRAD. Hey, sorry –

MELODY. Hey! It's okay, come in! How's it going?

BRAD. Good!

Just got grab this thing off / Craig's

MELODY. Yeah, he told me.

BRAD. We're working on this huge merger and then maybe I'll sleep?

MELODY. Overrated!

BRAD. So where's the –

MELODY. Oh, upstairs. On the left.

(**BRAD** *goes upstairs.*)

(**MELODY** *goes back to her mat, stretches. Aware of her shape, her pose.*)

(**BRAD** *comes back downstairs. Watches her stretch. He exhales. Clears his throat.*)

BRAD. Hey – so – I'm done –

(**MELODY** *gets out of her pose.*)

MELODY. Oh, cool!

BRAD. Have you guys tried Bikram?

MELODY. Not yet but I totally want to!

BRAD. There's a *great* center downtown.

MELODY. Yeah?

BRAD. Yeah and it's so, so intense. The sweat – *mobilizes* you. You're slippery like a baby. And you go through the things, and time flies and you come out at the end and it's like you've been fucking or crying for eight years.

MELODY. That sounds amazing!

BRAD. Yeah it totally is.

(beat)

I really liked talking to you. At that thing.

MELODY. Yeah me too!

BRAD. God I hate those things.

MELODY. Me *too!* Well at first I'm like, yay, excuse to wear a dress! But then an hour in my feet hurt and everyone's talking about refinancing their mortgages and I'm just really confused.

Craig bought this house, isn't that crazy?

BRAD. *So* crazy.

MELODY. *(smiling)* I got a little drunk at the thing.

BRAD. A little?

MELODY. I got medium a lot drunk.

BRAD. Me too. Um, we were wasted.

MELODY. Yes! Yes we were!

BRAD. It's the only way to make it through those things without inexplicably bursting into tears or killing yourself.

MELODY. Totally.

I was thinking the other day about that thing you said. About Tibetan Buddhists?

BRAD. Ah! You remember!

MELODY. I remember some parts! Of our conversation!

BRAD. Yeah about how they – um – contemplate their own deaths on a daily basis.

MELODY. Yeah and then this makes them less afraid.

BRAD. Yeah –

MELODY. That's so powerful –

BRAD. I watched a documentary online. I don't personally know any Tibetan Buddhists.

MELODY. That's okay!

BRAD. So you stoked for Craig to come back? Tonight, right?

MELODY. Oh, yeah! Yes.

His flight was super delayed so.

BRAD. He's freaking out, isn't he?

MELODY. How'd you know?

BRAD. Once he was running like ten minutes late for a meeting and he almost had a panic attack.

MELODY. Yeah, he does that!

BRAD. He's a great guy. He's a great guy to work for.

(beat)

So you having a better time?

MELODY. What?

BRAD. At the party, you said *I hate it here* –

MELODY. I did?

BRAD. Yep –

MELODY. Nah, I'm fine.

It's just kind of – it's just hard to be so far from home. And it's – you know it's an okay town / but

BRAD. Whoa, don't talk shit about my hometown!

MELODY. Oh sorry

BRAD. I'm totally kidding, I fucking hate it here.

MELODY. I should give it a chance, I haven't given it much of chance.

BRAD. Everyone's pretty lame. I mean like really good people.

But lame.

MELODY. I should make friends.

BRAD. *(fucking with her)* Yeah you should.

MELODY. *(cute, kidding)* Will you be my friend?

BRAD. Maybe.

MELODY. We could go rollerskating.

BRAD. We could get drunk and then also go rollerskating.

MELODY. Well wait, what're you doing here if you don't like it?

BRAD. *(shrugging, slightly embarrassed)* Yeah – My dad's a partner at the firm – so –

MELODY. Ah –

BRAD. Yeah so he got me the job, it's just paralegal bullshit, I'm just – just trying to figure out what I really want to do. Then I'm out.

MELODY. You don't belong in an office, you belong on a *boat.*

BRAD. Like what kind of boat?

MELODY. Like a dingy, sailing around the world.

BRAD. How'd you know?

MELODY. I just do. Also, You're meant to grow a beard.

BRAD. I had the most EPIC beard, in college.

(beat)

MELODY. Guess what, I think I have a brain tumor!

BRAD. No shit! Don't die!

MELODY. I have this pain thing in my ear. This stabbing pain. I went to braintumor.org.

BRAD. What it'd say?

MELODY. *(kind of joking)* I don't think I have one really. If I did I'd be seizing.

BRAD. *(smiling with her)* I'm sure you don't.

MELODY. Craig thinks I'm crazy.

Welp. I should probably get 'dinner on.'

BRAD. What're you making?

MELODY. Oh by get dinner on I definitely meant call a foreigner and ask him or her to bring it to me in containers. That I feel really bad about throwing away.

BRAD. Yeah me too. It's like really wasteful.

MELODY. So I stack them in a cabinet and every time I open the cabinet and look at all the containers I kind of want to die.

I suck at taking care of him.

BRAD. He can take care of himself!

MELODY. That's what *I* say! But his freakin mom –

BRAD. Ah, I met her – total Mayberry –

MELODY. I know, right?!

But she hates me. Or I hate her. I don't even know anymore.

Oh my God why am I telling you this?

I feel like I haven't talked to anyone in real life in 3 days. Wait, I haven't.

BRAD. You can talk to me.

(Beat. **MELODY** *lets go.)*

MELODY. Ahhhhhhhh I don't know if it's just being HERE or –

He's got this hoodie. Like his undergrad hoodie. It's got parmesan cheese crusted on the cuffs and it smells like balls and he won't wash it.

MELODY. He makes jokes but they're like: *what's a guy gotta do around here to get a blowjob?* And he's kidding, but he's not, And I'm like *you're* a blowjob!

Honestly sometimes I'd kind of rather just watch TV.

BRAD. Personally I'd always pick the blowjob.

MELODY. Yeah you would.

BRAD. What?

MELODY. Ha. Um.

BRAD. I'm sure marriage is like – super intense.

MELODY. It is but it's good.

> *(beat)*

It's just different now.

> *(Beat.* **MELODY** *is getting upset, flooded with honesty.)*

I look at him and it's like: who're you? Who is this person I sleep next to every night? You know what I mean?

BRAD. Totally.

MELODY. Do you have / a

BRAD. No but I totally know what you mean. About intimacy.

MELODY. You wanna get married?

BRAD. *(kidding)* You're married to my boss – awkward –

MELODY. No I mean in GENERAL.

BRAD. No, I mean maybe, like in my 30's or 40's? Once I'm ready?

MELODY. Yeah.

BRAD. Emotionally prepared.

> *(beat)*

Not that you're *not* like ready I didn't / mean

MELODY. No, I know.

BRAD. Well I guess I better head out –

MELODY. Hey you know anything about cable boxes?

BRAD. Maybe?

MELODY. My 'box' is broken. Ha! I'm funny.

BRAD. Yeah you are!

(**BRAD** *laughs.*)

Let's see here –

(*He puts down his stuff, crouches in front of the TV.*)

I think we just gotta re-boot it – this little button – c'mere, see?

(**MELODY** *joins him.*)

(*He presses a button. They sit close together, looking at the box.*)

(**BRAD** *looks at her.*)

(*They look at each other. A moment. Will they kiss? Seriously? But - the cable box pops back on. Sound of bad TV.*)

(**BRAD** *pulls away, clears his throat.*)

Ahhhh – well –

You just gotta reboot the box, if it does that –

MELODY. Okay..........

(*They both stand.*)

BRAD. (*with voice*) I don't think you'll be having any future interruptions. Ma'am.

MELODY. Thanks – cable man, sir –

(*beat*)

BRAD. I should / probably go

MELODY. You don't have to –

BRAD. Yeah but I probably should.

(**BRAD** *goes.* **MELODY** *sits on the couch. Looks at her phone. She turns back to the TV. Flips channels. Stops.*)

(**MELODY**'s *eyes focus on the TV screen. They grow wide. Bigger than wide. She puts a hand to her mouth.*)

Oh my God – Oh my God Oh my God –

(*She reaches for her phone.*)

(From the TV:)

NEWS. *(droning)* At least 50 passengers were killed when a commuter plane originating in Chicago crashed into a home in the suburbs of Albany. The crash occurred just moments after the pilots lost communication with air traffic controllers. The aircraft began a sudden nosedive just after 9:30 pm, then hit a home and burst into flames, according to witnesses.

MELODY. Please pick up Craig please pick up –

(MELODY *remains, crouched in front of the TV, eyes glued to the flickering footage.)*

(Night falls.)

(The sound of an airplane crashing into a house.)

(MELODY *stays glued to the TV, sitting in front of it in a crumpled mess on the floor.)*

(She can't take her eyes off of it.)

(She sobs, or tries, but it gets stuck in her throat.)

(She scoots closer to the TV, watches, obsessed.)

(The sun comes up.)

(HOPE, *poised but damaged, comes in through the front door.)*

*(She spots **MELODY**.)*

(goes to her, pulls her to her feet)

(MELODY *is limp.* **HOPE** *helps her stand.)*

(MELODY *leans on* **HOPE,** *starts to sob.* **HOPE** *lets this happen, pats her gingerly.)*

*(pulls **MELODY** away from her, pushes hair out of her face)*

(HOPE *leads* **MELODY** *offstage.)*

(HOPE *returns and surveys the room. Begins to clean.)*

III.

(The living room, later the next day. **HOPE** *sits on the couch. She is a bit somber, but poised. She has a neat legal pad with a massive list.)*

HOPE. I've booked First Presbyterian for Sunday.

Good thing they were free. It's a lovely church, there's a real pipe organ. A place by the altar where folks can donate flowers. Lilies, azaleas.

The pastor, it was his father that baptized Craig.

(A moment. **HOPE** *starts to cry because no one is looking. She stops. She clears her throat. She tries to relate to* **MELODY**.*)*

We *would* be picking out the casket, his best suit.

With Craig's father he had gotten – he had gotten so THIN I – I had a new one made.

But there's –

there's not as much to do *now* with no body.

It's – it's unfortunate.

That there won't be a body.

*(***MELODY*** *emerges in an awful black dress. Her eyes are red but her chin is high. She is stunned.)*

MELODY. Is this black black enough?

Is it gray, or is it black?

HOPE. Yes. That's black.

MELODY. I feel like a lesbian.

HOPE. It's not the prom, dear.

MELODY. This is my first funeral.

It's the only funeral I've ever been to.

HOPE. That dress will suffice.

(back to her list)

We'll have the lunch at my home after the service.

MELODY. Shouldn't we have it here?

HOPE. Dear, really, are you in any shape to host a lunch? Please, let / me

MELODY. Craig loved this house. This is his house.

HOPE. But my house is much more central for the guests.

MELODY. He'd want to do it here.

(beat)

HOPE. Fine.

I'll have the cleaners come by Saturday so we should straighten up first.

MELODY. What do we do now?

HOPE. Well we have a service to plan.

Did you speak with your parents?

MELODY. They're trying to get a flight – they got four feet of snow, the airports closed –

HOPE. Hopefully they'll make it by Sunday.

MELODY. Can we wait for them? If they can't –

HOPE. I'm sorry but it can't wait.

(beat)

We have to do it Sunday. It's the only day the church is available.

MELODY. I can make a playlist. For the service. I've been making it in my head, the songs he liked –

(She goes to grab it. It's a bright blue to her pink.)

HOPE. I've already hired an organist.

MELODY. Maybe we could put out all of the candies and stuff he liked, Little Debbie nutty bars! Skittles! And sour patch kids!

HOPE. Craig doesn't eat trash like that.

MELODY. Um, yes he did. Those are his favorites. He hid them in his car.

HOPE. *(flustered)* You can't serve CANDY at a funeral. What would people think?

MELODY. They'd be like: yay! Candy!

HOPE. The caterer will handle the food, I've already placed the order.

(Beat. **MELODY** *reaches for pen / paper.)*

MELODY. I'm going to work on my speech.

HOPE. Your what?

MELODY. For the funeral.

HOPE. A eulogy....

It's not expected of the Widow.

MELODY. Yeah but – but I *want* to.

HOPE. I've asked the pastor to say a few words.

MELODY. What're you doing, can I help with what you're doing?

HOPE. I'm making a list of everyone who needs to be notified.

*(**MELODY** peers over her shoulder.)*

MELODY. I don't know any of these people.

HOPE. Well they knew Craig.

MELODY. I can call people.

HOPE. I have friends through the League who can take care of the calls.

MELODY. No I can do it.

I can call people in Boulder. His. The people I know.

(She grabs her phone. Scrolls through. Dials.)

HOPE. Melody –

MELODY. No it's okay I can do this, this is good –

HOPE. You don't need to do this.

Melody hang up the phone. MELODY.

MELODY. *(on phone)* Hey Jimmy?

What's up it's Melody –

How's it going?

I'm okay.

Ha – cool –

Listen um –

Craig is dead.

(She pauses, regains herself.)

MELODY. He was on that plane that crashed –

Okay I'll talk to you later bye!!!!

(She hangs up, tosses the phone like it's on fire.)

I can't do this –

(She loses it. She sobs.)

When do I get to see him?

HOPE. Melody.

MELODY. I wanna see him, where is he?

HOPE. He's gone.

MELODY. HOW DO WE KNOW?!

HOPE. It is – it's unfortunate. With no body.

MELODY. I don't even – we don't even get to – we don't even know where he IS.

HOPE. Melody. Listen to me.

There's a way things are meant to happen. In these – times.

First and foremost you have to keep yourself together.

MELODY. How?!

HOPE. I'll take your dress and iron it.

Try and keep it lint free and pressed. Try and keep a lint roller nearby.

MELODY. I don't – have one –

MELODY. An inside piece of packing tape will do.

MELODY. I don't know how to do this. Oh my God.

HOPE. I want to hug you. Come on now. Let's hug.

(**MELODY** *reluctantly goes towards* **HOPE**. *They embrace.* **HOPE** *holds her a bit stiffly.*)

MELODY. I can't stop – I can't stop wondering like or SEEING like – what was going through his head when he – did it hurt him, did he hurt?!

HOPE. He's in heaven now. Playing cards with his father.

(**MELODY** *settles into* **HOPE**'s *embrace.*)

MELODY. But I don't know if I even believe in heaven. I haven't decided yet.

HOPE. You haven't *decided?*

(There is a knock at the door.)

Mourners. So persistent.

(yelling to door)

WE AREN'T CURRENTLY RECEIVING!

*(**MELODY** goes to the door, opens it to find **BRAD**, disheveled and beside himself – but with an air of tragic hero.)*

*(**MELODY** freezes when she sees him. He looks deliciously sad but she tries to not notice this.)*

BRAD. Oh my God, Melody – I just heard – I came right over –

MELODY. Hi –

*(**MELODY** indicates **HOPE**.)*

BRAD. Oh – hi – sorry –

MELODY. Um, Hope, You remember Brad, he works at Craig's firm.

This is Craig's mother. Hope.

BRAD. Hello. *(beat)* I'm deeply um – sorry for your loss.

HOPE. *(bowing her head gracefully)* That's very kind of you. And I'm sorry for yours.

BRAD. Thank you. It's not as big as yours.

HOPE. Probably not.

BRAD. But it's pretty big.

*(to **MELODY**)*

When I saw it on the news I couldn't believe it, I kept thinking or hoping maybe he had *missed* the plane like maybe he had too much bourbon at the bar or a flat tire or maybe he was taking a shit and they called his name over and over.

Sorry.

MELODY. He would never miss the plane.

HOPE. He was very punctual, that's how I raised him.

BRAD. I know.

MELODY. I know, too.

HOPE. I also know.

(They look at each other.)

BRAD. He was um – I want you to know he was kind of like a big brother to me.

So you're kind of like my Mom.

I know you're not my Mom but.

He was like my brother.

HOPE. Thank you.

*(**HOPE** nods. **MELODY** is like, what the fuck.)*

BRAD. I want to help. There's a lot to do, there are things we need to –

HOPE. I've – Melody, we've – got everything under control.

BRAD. What do you need? I will literally do anything for you right now. Literally.

HOPE. That's very sweet of you.

BRAD. I'd be honored to – speak a poem at the service.

Psalm 23.

Or John Donne. 'Death be not proud –'

Or Walt Whitman, *Song of Myself.*

"Failing to fetch me at first keep encouraged – Missing me one place search another – I stop somewhere waiting for you."

(beat)

Those are just suggestions.

HOPE. That's very kind of you, Bob / but the service has already been planned.

BRAD. Brad – There's all the stuff at – all of his, um – his stuff, at his office, um, like his stapler and his, he has a drawer full of Tylenol and really nice hand lotions and I don't think he'd want me to throw them away and I should probably – Jesus – Jesus Christ –

(He chokes up.)

And there's this really big jar of Swedish fish –

MELODY. *(softly, weirdly)* Asshole –

BRAD. And his books – and his things –

HOPE. We'll sort it all out after the funeral.

BRAD. Just – if you need anything – you can call me – any time.

MELODY. *(quickly)* I won't.

BRAD. But if you do.

HOPE. Thank you for coming.

>   *(**MELODY** nods. **BRAD** goes. **HOPE** studies **MELODY**.)*

HOPE. Well he's nice young man.

MELODY. I really don't know him all that well.

>   *(beat)*

HOPE. Mourning is a *private* affair.

>   *(She looks at **MELODY**, her smeared make up.)*

>   Oh my goodness – you're a mess –

>   *(She wets a thumb and roughly rubs mascara off of **MELODY**'s face.)*

>   Dear, you are a widow now –

MELODY. I KNOW

HOPE. Oh my – so much eye make up –

MELODY. I'm not your daughter.

HOPE. *(under her breath)* Thank God.

>   *(Suddenly, **MELODY** spots **CRAIG** out the window.)*

>   *(He waves to her.)*

>   *(She waves back.)*

>   *(**HOPE** returns to her list.)*

>   *(**CRAIG** is gone.)*

IV.

(**MELODY**, *late that night, alone in the house, still wearing the frumpy black dress. Over it, the crusty hoodie.*)

(*She has a pen and legal pad. Her eyes are shut, tight, she is thinking, so hard.*)

(*She listens to the remnants of Craig, his last voicemail, over and over. We hear them.*
I love you. Oh, it's Craig.
I love you. Oh, it's Craig.
I love you. Oh, it's Craig.)

(*She stops herself. Puts on music, Willie Nelson from Craig's blue iPod, Low.*)

(*Her eyes burst open. She writes.*)

MELODY. He was a person – who –

What kind of person was he? What kind of person is *anyone?*

Survived by his wife Melody. 26 years of age. 26 years old.

Also survived by his mother, Hope, fifty something. Of Connecticut. His father, Frank, died when he was young. Of cancer?

Craig was a corporate lawyer. He merged and – purchased things.

(*Beat. She closes her eyes and listens to the music.*)

He liked….

He liked coconut cake very much? No, Red Velvet better.

Also, he liked Willie Nelson and Seinfeld re-runs. He makes the best Fettuccine Alfredo.

And when he makes it he – (*she smiles, starts to laugh*) he does this thing he's like – FETTUCINE MONSTERR and I'm like FETTUCINE MONSTERRRRR

(*She laughs. She stops.*)

He liked Boxer briefs and he folded them.

My underwear is in bunches in a drawer. Next to his folded.

It's so weird. To know someone.

He has no hair on his back or shoulders. His hair recedes one millimeter a year. Sometimes if he can't get it up you have to put your face on his stomach or call him Papi.

He doesn't like Brussels sprouts or pearl onions, he thinks they're like eyes.

He is the nicest man. He is the nicest, nicest man and he has the nicest, nicest hands that anyone would be so lucky to be all wrapped up in.

Had.

Had the nicest hands.

(beat)

I knew him but I didn't but I did.

But I loved him.

I think.

We loved each other.

(beat)

When he asked me to marry him –

I said – I said yes.

(She stops. She can barely breathe. She smiles, remembering.)

*(**CRAIG** turns on the light. **MELODY** is there waiting.)*

Surprisseeeeeeeeeeee

CRAIG. How'd you get in here?!

MELODY. I'm sneaky. Told the guy at the front desk that I was your misses and that I lost my key card.

CRAIG. Liar.

MELODY. You okay?

CRAIG. Yeah, just – Today was freaking NUTS.

MELODY. How so?

CRAIG. Just a lot.

Going on. Hold on sorry –

MELODY. It's okay, You can do work and ALSO pay attention to me.

CRAIG. Yes. *(Blackberry.)* I. *(Blackberry.)* Can.

(tosses it)

Fini!!!

MELODY. Oui oui!

CRAIG. I thought you were going out tonight?

MELODY. It felt stupid all the sudden. "Going out."
Also I'm sick of my roommates. I'm sick of roommates.
I like it better here.

CRAIG. It's getting old.
I want like a "home." I wanna put stuff on the walls, I
wanna leave my things somewhere.

MELODY. Can I come?

CRAIG. Sure you can.

MELODY. Yay, can I wear an apron? Can it have cats on it?

CRAIG. You bet.

(She burrows into his hoodie.)

Ah! I see you found my sweatshirt.

MELODY. It's mine now, I'm cold!

*(**MELODY** yawns, burrowing into **CRAIG**.)*

(He moves.)

CRAIG. Are you serious?

MELODY. Maybe, about what?

CRAIG. About being sick of roommates –

MELODY. Uh yes. If you're going to fight with somebody
about who's taking the trash out you should at least
also be having sex with them.

*(**CRAIG** laughs. Looks at her with intensity.)*

…What?

CRAIG. I uh – I got this job offer, I um – in Connecticut –

MELODY. Well are you gonna take it?

CRAIG. Well you know I've been wanting to get back closer
to my mom eventually / and –

MELODY. Yeah –

CRAIG. What if you came with me?

MELODY. To Connecticut?

Like – ?

CRAIG. We could actually live together! Like in a house! Like normal people!

MELODY. Yeah!

(**CRAIG** *pulls a ring box out of his pocket.*)

CRAIG. So I was thinking – so – I got you this –

MELODY. I look like shit right now –

CRAIG. Melody, will you marry me?

(**MELODY** *tears.*)

I had this whole – thing – planned, but you don't need a thing, and now just seemed like the right –

MELODY. No, this is perfect!

CRAIG. So – will you –

MELODY. Yes! Yes!

(**CRAIG** *pulls her to her sock-ed feet.*)

(*He hugs her. He holds her.*)

CRAIG. Are you freaking out?

MELODY. No! – I mean we haven't even talked / about it. Sorry, it's just kind of, but YAY!

CRAIG. You happy?

MELODY. Yeah!

How long have you had the ring?

CRAIG. It was my grandma's. You like it?

MELODY. It's so pretty!

CRAIG. Really, you like it?

MELODY. I love it.

CRAIG. (*nuzzling her*) My fiancée –

MELODY. I'm a fiancée!!

(*They kiss.*)

Can we do it again? Do over – do over –

I didn't show you enough. How excited I was. That wasn't enough.

MELODY. Come on, ask me again.

I'm very excited!

(**CRAIG** *snaps back into pre-proposal position, on one knee.*)

CRAIG. Melody, will you / marry me?

MELODY. YES I WILL MARRY YOU!

Sorry – that was –

One more time? sorry –

(*Lights shift again.* **CRAIG** *gets to one knee.*)

CRAIG. Melody, will you marry me?

(**MELODY** *hesitates.*)

MELODY. Why did you? Ask me? Was it because of me, or?

(**CRAIG** *carries on with post-proposal.*)

CRAIG. You hungry?

MELODY. It was like: "Hey Mel, what's up. Oh, I was wondering, would you marry me?" "Golly, sure!"

CRAIG. What do we need, do we need cake?

MELODY. "May wedding sound good?"

"Yay, May!"

CRAIG. We need waffles. Chocolate chip waffles.

MELODY. "Then we'll start trying for kids – year after?"

"Naturally!"

"Perfect. Cause after I make partner, I'm gonna need some kids."

CRAIG. I can't wait to tell my Mom!

(**CRAIG** *moves towards the stairs.*)

MELODY. Where're you going?

CRAIG. Run a bath!

MELODY. You wanna take a bath right now? You're ruining this –

CRAIG. For *us.*

MELODY. No – not yet –

Stay here with me – let me look at you!

CRAIG. Calm down, I'll just be in the bathroom!

MELODY. No I wanna be where *you* are!

CRAIG. Then come with me!

MELODY. I CAN'T.

(**CRAIG** *is gone. Lights shift back to normal.*)

Craig –

(*The house is quiet.*)

(*She tries to shake this off. She thinks of something.*)

(*She grabs her car keys and goes.*)

(*Sirens, flashing lights, smoke and fire, far away.*)

V.

(The living room, later that night. The house is a mess.)

*(**HOPE** is trying to clean up. You know, for the cleaners.)*

*(**MELODY** sits on the couch, in a daze. She's an even bigger mess.)*

HOPE. You do realize I have more important things to be do than pick you up from the police station in the middle of the night?

Why on *earth* did you go there?! Why?!

MELODY. I needed to see.

HOPE. Why would you want to see that???

MELODY. I thought he would be there but he wasn't. There were shoes and there were bags and there were bones but none of it was HIM.

HOPE. You should take a shower, you stink.

MELODY. The fires were still burning.

HOPE. What did you expect?!

MELODY. The house it crashed into, pictures and books and smoke and limbs –

HOPE. *(dismissing, covering)* Well now I've lost my appetite.

MELODY. There were these ropes around the whole thing.

HOPE. Because people are not supposed to BE THERE, Melody. You are not supposed to SEE THAT.

MELODY. But I went right through the ropes and I said *I need to see my husband!* They said *you can't be here* I said I'M A WIDOW.

HOPE. You're certainly not acting like one.

MELODY. I could see the tail – and the nose. I went to the tail. It was as big as a boat but it was also it was tiny like the end of a match. See Craig was in the back. I checked his ticket confirmation. Seat 31A. I thought maybe there would be a carry-on or a sweater or anything he ate half of?

MELODY. *(cont.)* The trees were moving but there was no wind. And all over the ground, *everywhere,*
I saw – pieces of people. Guts on the shoes of the workers. I saw an arm – it wasn't Craig's arm

HOPE. You *mustn't* – we must focus on the tasks at HAND.

MELODY. Each piece of a person has a family – and so then, where are they now?! Where is each person now?! Where did they go?!

HOPE. Help me clean up before the cleaners come.

MELODY. People put into bags like leftovers. Craig pieced back together put into these bags. Pieces of him I never knew or saw. It must have hurt – it must have hurt so much!

HOPE. *(about to lose it)* Please – *stop.*

MELODY. We FEEL like we are strong, I FEEL like I'm indestructible, I never thought about this but we are about as strong as grass. We can get RIPPED apart. He was RIPPED apart. Before I could even –

HOPE. Stop it.

MELODY. I smelled skin burning and now it's stuck in my nose. It's stuck in my eyes!!!

HOPE. WE WON'T DISCUSS IT.

MELODY. Don't you miss him?!

(beat)

HOPE. I understand what you're going through, I *really* do but – *(beat)* It's important that you just *own* it. Your grief. Wear it like a brassiere, like something you'd wear every day.

MELODY. I don't wear a bra everyday.

HOPE. MY POINT IS, It's important you don't use it to justify irrational behavior. There are rules.
When I lost my husband they were very useful.

*(***MELODY*** *sobs.)*

MELODY. I want my mom – I want my mom and my dad.

HOPE. They're not going to be here forever.

MELODY. Yes – I know I just this I just I've never lost any-body before!

HOPE. You have to try and keep it together.

MELODY. I feel like getting drunk.

HOPE. It doesn't help. Trust me, it doesn't drown, it accen-tuates.

I was looking in your kitchen.

You're going to need some sturdy non-stick pans.

For Bundt cakes, for funerals, after other deaths.

There will be other funerals. I've gotten you a mem-bership with the Widow's League, it's a valuable resource. It's very important to have fellowship with other widows.

(beat)

MELODY. These 'rules' work for you?

HOPE. YES.

MELODY. *How,* how do they work?!

HOPE. They provide great comfort.

MELODY. You don't seem very comfortable.

HOPE. I – I am just trying to keep it *together.*

MELODY. So am I but it's HARD.

HOPE. Oh, it's hard for *you?* It's hard.

Melody you have NO idea what you're talking about. You have NO CONCEPT of the – of what it takes!

MELODY. What WHAT takes?!

HOPE. Honoring your husband after his death.

And before it.

MELODY. I TRIED.

HOPE. You have NO idea.

MELODY. I'm sorry you don't like me / I'm really sorry, but Craig married ME, and I married HIM and

HOPE. I don't not *like* you! I just doubt your ability to take care of him!

MELODY. No, you're right. I was a shitty wife, I'm a shitty widow.

HOPE. Melody –

MELODY. No, your son and my husband is DEAD and you want to pick lint off my dress?! Fuck your rules.

You're not even remembering him you're not even THINKING about him.

HOPE. YOU SHUT YOUR FUCKING FACE.

(A tiny glimpse into the depth of her pain.)

*(**MELODY** has no idea what to do.)*

(beat)

I'll be by Sunday morning. We must arrive together in the limo.

There's a song.

It is well.

It is well, it is well, with my soul.

A man wrote it after his wife and four daughters sank on a boat, and died.

His whole family.

Think about *that,* Melody.

*(**HOPE** is gone.)*

*(**MELODY** goes for vodka.)*

VI.

(Later that night. The living room.)

*(**MELODY** has been drinking vodka. A small, sad party of one.)*

(She's wearing her dress as a skirt. Fortunately, she's still wearing a bra.)

(LOUD music shakes the walls, coming from Craig's iPod. She is dancing.)

(A knock on the door.)

MELODY. Craig?

(The knocks persist.)

Let yourself in, ghost.

(A door shuts.)

*(**BRAD** enters, disheveled, with bike helmet.)*

You're not my husband.

BRAD. I know. It's Brad.

MELODY. You shouldn't be here.

BRAD. You called me.

MELODY. I did?

BRAD. Yeah.

MELODY. What'd I say?

BRAD. "Come over."

MELODY. I'M AWESOME.

BRAD. I rode my bike over. I haven't ridden my bike in forever. I was like: *I need to ride my bike right now.*

MELODY. I had a bike, I miss my bike. I left it in Colorado.

BRAD. These last few days have felt like *years.*

I went to take a shit and I was like, *why?*

I don't know what to do with myself.

MELODY. You're not allowed to be sad cause no one is sad as *me.* I'm the *widow.*

BRAD. You're sad.

MELODY. Say I'm sadder than you.

BRAD. You're sadder.

MELODY. Do I look like a widow?

BRAD. Totally –

MELODY. I'm *really* good at it, I know all the rules.
Like the one about how you probably shouldn't be here right now.

BRAD. I shouldnt've ridden over. I've been drinking. I killed like half a bottle of this really nice chianti I've been saving, I almost hit a pole coming over, I ALMOST DIED, my mind isn't right. I should probably just stay here.

MELODY. You can stay but don't fucking touch me or I'll scream.

BRAD. Okay.

(**BRAD** *comes in, takes off his shoes.* **MELODY** *gives him a drink.* **BRAD** *takes a piece of paper out of his pocket, looks at it.*)

MELODY. What's that?

BRAD. I wrote a poem. For Craig, for the service, it's really bad.

MELODY. Can I hear it?

BRAD. It's really bad.

MELODY. I wanna hear it.

BRAD. *(reciting, seriously, vulnerably)* 'A poem for Craig.'

(long pause)

Craig –
You were my friend
Until the end.
And your end
My friend
Came much too soon.
When I saw the news
I was adding ones and twos
With my calculator.

BRAD. I was doing a report for you.

> Through doing I found meaning.
> Meaning being the reality of doing,
> And doing things for You,
> Was Good.
> I didn't always like it but I found
> Harmony there,
> In the doing.

> And I stopped what I was doing
> And looked and saw and
> I felt you fall and I fell to the ground and
> My lunch came up in my throat and
> My calculator fell onto the carpet.
> Like you fell.

> *(beat)*

> So that's the end.

> (**MELODY** *is moved, connected to him.*)

MELODY. I saw the crash. I went and I saw it.

BRAD. Are you serious? You shouldn't have seen that shit.

MELODY. I did.

BRAD. Why'd you do it?

MELODY. I needed to.

BRAD. *(getting it)* Part of your process…

MELODY. Yeah.

BRAD. What was it like?

MELODY. It was awful.

BRAD. Like what?

MELODY. Like a massacre – and this smell – You ever wonder, *what does a dead body smell like?*

BRAD. Yes –

MELODY. It smells like animals.

BRAD. Like what kind of animal?

MELODY. Like a petting zoo maybe but with fire and blood –

BRAD. Can I tell you something, can I be totally honest?

MELODY. YES

BRAD. I used to like it when he was out of town. Oh God –

MELODY. *(needing to talk)* Me too, I mean I missed him when he was gone but I used to like the alone time –

I like Poptarts for dinner and a lot of *Project Runway*.

BRAD. Who's your favorite?

MELODY. Bridget.

BRAD. I like Clive.

MELODY. He's okay.

BRAD. He was so he was so good to me – I mean he worked me hard but it was because he cared but I would like RESENT him sometimes when he just asked me to DO something. And it's my JOB to do things for him, that's my JOB.

MELODY. I wanna wake up like it never happened.

I want him to walk in the door.

BRAD. Did you ever wonder – what if there was a way I could go to my own funeral?

MELODY. Yes.

BRAD. Me too.

(**MELODY** *changes the song to something hard and DMX.*)

MELODY. You wanna dance?

BRAD. What kind?

MELODY. Like a party.

His running mix.

Apparently when he was running he liked to feel like he could kill people.

(She starts to dance, letting the music move her. It's sloppy and hot. **BRAD** *joins her. They are grief-dancing.)*

(They are grinding and sweating, dancing.)

*(***BRAD*** starts to move his hands over her.)*

MELODY. This is bad – this is so against the rules –

> (**MELODY** *grabs hold of* **BRAD**, *hugs him, hard, needing to be held.*)

> (**BRAD** *puts his arms around her.*)

BRAD. It's okay, I got you –
Here I am –

> (**BRAD** *holds her tighter.*)

> (**BRAD** *kisses* **MELODY**. *For a moment, she kisses him back desperately.*)

> (*They go for it, hard, and it's hot.*)

> (*turned on*) Shit –

> (**MELODY** *stops, pulls herself away. Tries to get her bearings.*)

MELODY. Craig –

BRAD. What?
You okay Mel?

MELODY. Don't call me that.

BRAD. Sorry –

> (**MELODY** *brings her hands to her lips. To her gut. She sits on the couch.*)

MELODY. Sorry, I'm sorry.
I think maybe you should go.

BRAD. Okay, are you sure?

> (**MELODY** *nods.*)

I don't know if you should be alone right now.

MELODY. No, I want to be.

BRAD. Maybe we could be alone but like also together.

MELODY. We shouldn't be doing ANYTHING right now
Brad, we are fucking crazy right now –

BRAD. I love you, I think –

> (**CRAIG** *laughs.*)

MELODY. What?!

We can't do this.

We're grown ass adults I think. No, I know.

BRAD. I'm not immature. I am very mature.

(He heads for the door and is gone.)

(beat)

*(**CRAIG** enters.)*

MELODY. You came home!!!

CRAIG. I did!

MELODY. He made it!! He finally made it!

CRAIG. Gahhhh that took forever.

*(**MELODY** takes his suitcase, kisses him.)*

Did you get my / message

MELODY. I was a bitch on the phone, I'm so sorry

CRAIG. I too was a bitch!

MELODY. Seriously, I'm sorry.

CRAIG. Me too.

MELODY. I love it when you tell me you love me.

I don't care how many times you tell me.

(She kisses him.)

How was the flight?

CRAIG. You know, the plane was on the ground, then it finally took off, then it was in the air, then on the ground again, it was pretty standard.

*(**MELODY** laughs.)*

MELODY. Uch, I don't know how you do it so much, I hate flying.

CRAIG. White wine, Sinatra, and Tylenol PM.

MELODY. Oh, you're drunk?

CRAIG. Sobered up. Ate some nuts.

MELODY. Hahahaha –

(They both laugh.)

Guess what I had lunch with your mom!

CRAIG. Aww!

MELODY. Yeah we're going to take a gardening class together. I think we're best friends.

CRAIG. That's great!

MELODY. Yeah and also, I made chili and also, I missed you.

CRAIG. Mmmm feels good to be home.

*(***CRAIG*** grabs her.)*

MELODY. I missed you.

CRAIG. Me too.

(She kisses him.)

MELODY. You must be starved.

*(***CRAIG*** sits foreignly on the couch, removes his shoes. He looks around the room like he doesn't belong. He turns on the TV. He watches the news.)*

CRAIG. Oh shit, a plane crashed!

*(***MELODY,*** now wearing an apron, sauced spoon in hand, pokes her head in.)*

MELODY. What?

CRAIG. A plane crashed –

MELODY. *(Her eyes focus on the TV. They watch together for a minute.)* You want a salad too?

CRAIG. That'd be great.

(at news)

It's all over everywhere. It *crashed.* That's terrifying, wow.

*(She sits with him. They watch the carnage. ***CRAIG*** is engrossed.)*

At least I wasn't on it right?

MELODY. Yes. You were.

What am I doing….What am I *doing…*

*(***CRAIG*** goes.)*

*(***MELODY*** *alone in the house. The room seems to brighten. She sees the mess she's made.)*

(She straightens up the house. Pulls herself together.)

VII.

(The living room. The morning of the funeral.)

(The doorbell rings.)

(Doorbell rings again. Cautiously, self consciously, **BRAD** *lets himself in.)*

(He stands uncomfortably in the living room with an elaborate bouquet of begonias.)

*(***MELODY*** enters.)*

(She is a radiant, well-dressed widow in a black dress pressed with grief. She has pulled herself together. Almost too together. Stiff.)

BRAD. Good morning.

MELODY. What're you doing here?

BRAD. I'm sorry – the door was open –

MELODY. This is my house. You can't just let yourself into my house.

I'm about to bury my husband.

I have a party to prepare for. A lunch.

BRAD. I just wanted to give you these flowers before the – I mean I'll be at church but these are just for you.

(He holds them out to her. She takes them, frowns at them.)

They're begonias. They're symbolic of balance and psychism.

MELODY. They don't go with the rest of the flowers.

BRAD. They're for you.

*(***MELODY*** gives flowers back.)*

MELODY. They don't match. Thank you, but they don't match.

BRAD. You're missing the point.

I wanted to um – apologize.

MELODY. Nothing happened.

BRAD. Why're you being like this?

MELODY. *(proudly)* I'll see you at the service.

BRAD. I just wanted to say, I like – feel for you.

MELODY. Brad –

BRAD. I don't know if it's 'for' you it might also be something selfish, which is my least favorite thing, selfishness, even though everything I do turns out to be selfish and I really hate that.

MELODY. I can't handle this right now.

BRAD. Just – are you okay?

MELODY. Yeah.

BRAD. You promise?

(beat)

MELODY. Yeah.

BRAD. I'll see you at the church.

You don't have to like talk to me or anything but I'll be there.

*(**HOPE** enters, bedraggled and numb. She heads straight for the couch.)*

MELODY. Thanks.

BRAD. Good morning, again.

*(**BRAD** goes.)*

*(**MELODY** looks at **HOPE**. Something's terribly wrong.)*

MELODY. Good / morning –

HOPE. No it's not.

MELODY. He just – he just came by to bring flowers.

*(**HOPE** doesn't respond.)*

I'm so sorry about yesterday, I –

HOPE. Forgotten.

MELODY. No. It's not. I was completely inappropriate.

Do you like my dress? I got a new one. I wanted something a little longer / so I

HOPE. Melody –

MELODY. It's from Talbotts.

HOPE. Melody, you can stop.

Let's just get through today. Then you can live your life, and I can live what's left of mine.

MELODY. I don't want that.

I finished my eulogy.

I loved Craig. I loved him very very much.

(**HOPE** *looks like she could sleep for a hundred years. Or die.*)

HOPE. You have him still.

MELODY. What?

HOPE. You have him.

MELODY. So do you.

HOPE. No I don't.

I tried to – last night I –

I couldn't get it out my head.

The fire – and and the limbs –

MELODY. I'm so sorry I shouldn't / have

HOPE. So I –

I said *Hello Craig* but –

And he was in my dream and – and I didn't even know what to say to him! I couldn't say a word! When I opened my mouth, there was sand!

I have nothing.

MELODY. That's not true.

HOPE. No grandchildren.

MELODY. That's not – (*She stops, because it's true.*)

HOPE. I lost my husband and that was terrible but that was fine. Well it wasn't fine but I did it, I got through it for CRAIG, because he needed me and I couldn't be a wreck, he needed someone to get him out of bed in the morning, and I needed HIM to get me out of bed in the morning, and I don't even remember what Frank smelled like anymore but this is FINE, because I have CRAIG, and now he's GONE.

HOPE. *(cont.)* There's no word for a woman who looses their husband AND their son.

I forgot how to brush my teeth.

This morning I forgot how to brush my teeth.

So I didn't.

MELODY. It's okay to be sad.

> *(Beat.* **HOPE** *starts to break down.* **MELODY** *has no idea what to do. She peeks out the window.)*
>
> *(Limo honks.)*

The limo's here –

HOPE. I can't do this – I don't know if I can do this –

Look at me – I'm a mess –

MELODY. It's okay.

HOPE. No it's not –

MELODY. It is.

> *(A moment.* **HOPE** *howls with grief, relief.)*
>
> *(***MELODY*** *watches.)*
>
> *(Slowly, moves towards her to comfort her.)*
>
> *(Lights shift to later.)*
>
> *(In the dark, a hymn:)*

MUSIC.

> *When peace like a river*
> *Attendeth my way*
> *When sorrows like sea billows roll*
>
> *Whatever my lot*
> *Thou hast taught me say*
> *It is well*
> *It is well*
> *With my soul*
>
> *It is well, It is well*
> *It is well, It is well*
> *With my soul*

VIII.

(**MELODY**, *in the living room, alone. Night.*)

(**HOPE** *enters and approaches* **MELODY**, *sits next to her.*)

(**MELODY** *is a bit more together.* **HOPE** *is a bit more relaxed.*)

HOPE. There are bowls of skittles everywhere.

MELODY. It's what he would've wanted.

(*beat*)

HOPE. (*admitting*) I love skittles!

MELODY. So did Craig!!!!

HOPE. I never let myself have them but I love them so much!!

(**HOPE** *decides, and eats skittles.*)

(**HOPE** *exhales, takes off her shoes.*)

Your parents –

MELODY. Yes, sorry, I know – they're loud –

HOPE. They're lovely.

(*Beat.* **MELODY** *smiles.*)

MELODY. Yeah, they're pretty great.

HOPE. I'm glad they made it in time.

MELODY. Me too.

HOPE. They've invited me to visit. They say I didn't spend enough time at the wedding.

MELODY. You didn't.

HOPE. I – I felt left out.

MELODY. Why?

(**HOPE** *shrugs, embarrassed.*)

HOPE. Your mom wants to feed me, she says I'm too thin. And your dad wants me to meet his chickens?

MELODY. You should go, you should totally go!!
They would really like that.
I would really like that.

(an uncomfortable beat)

HOPE. Your eulogy. It was – it was beautiful. I'm very impressed with you, Melody.

MELODY. Thank you.

*(**HOPE** nods. They sit there together. **HOPE** starts to get up.)*

HOPE. I should / make sure there's ice

MELODY. I already checked, we're good, I promise.

*(Beat. **HOPE** sits back down. **MELODY** starts to laugh.)*

HOPE. What?

MELODY. The other night – after you left – I stood in the kitchen in Craig's underwear and I ate a whole pie.

HOPE. A WHOLE pie?

MELODY. Seriously I killed it.

(beat)

Is it going to feel like this forever?

HOPE. Yes. In a way.

MELODY. *Forever* forever?

HOPE. It – shifts a bit.

MELODY. How so?

HOPE. Some days are better than others.

MELODY. What do we do now?

*(**HOPE** holds a hand out to **MELODY**.)*

What's this?

HOPE. Come now. Come here. It's important that you know this.

MELODY. What am I 'knowing?'

*(**MELODY** won't move, so **HOPE** goes to her and guides her to the center of the floor, positions her for a polite dance.)*

HOPE. You see, chances are, at some point in the future, a man is bound to ask you to dance.

It's their duty as men.

So you bow gracefully –

(**HOPE** *does so.* **MELODY** *then does, too.*)

HOPE. And you accept. Take his hand but don't ever hold too tight or squeeze it.

And then you dance.

If you start to think of your husband, and the way he held you, if tears come to your eyes, focus on something about the gentleman that is gross or unattractive and keep your eyes there.

I prefer the chin or neck, or a mole. Dance with him for the duration of the song, then say thank you.

Come on now, try and keep up –

(**HOPE** *teaches* **MELODY** *to dance.*)

Then take a moment and remember your husband.

MELODY. Like right there, or go into a bathroom / and

HOPE. Just for a moment, right there. Say hello to his memory.

Don't flog yourself, don't run through all the things you should have said just –

Look at this new person and maybe – tell him how you feel.

Tell him about Craig.

Then you should probably cry on him and see how he takes it.

If he takes it: let him take you to lunch.

(**MELODY** *smiles.*)

(**HOPE** *goes.*)

(*Lights shift to later.*)

(**MELODY**, *cleaning up after the party. Music plays softly. She turns it off. Stands there in total silence. Stands there, listening to the silence.*)

(**CRAIG** *appears.*)

CRAIG. First we pitched up at 31 degrees.

Then we pitched left at 45 degrees.

Finally we pitched right at 60 degrees, then dropped twelve hundred feet in about five seconds.

CRAIG. *(cont.)* I thought of you.

Then I realized I was hungry and the hunger felt really strange and then I realized it was fear. And I wondered how many times in my life have I eaten when really all I needed to do was say a prayer or talk to somebody?

Then I thought. *Mother.* Also, I should get my laptop out of my carry on and why didn't I take that baseball scholarship and what does God think of me?

Then I thought, Brad. Brad can't finish that research himself. I thought, Brad is going to fuck this up.

We were plummeting.

I didn't dare look out the window and see the inevitable.

Everyone was sobbing and yelling out names. *Fred, oh Fred! My baby, my baby! Mommy!*

Then I wanted a cigarette. Screw this, I'm smoking.

But I didn't have any. I've never smoked. Fear of death.

Then I thought, what's Melody doing?

Then I thought, what's Melody going to do?

Then: I love her. Then: Oh my God I love her.

*(**CRAIG** looks at **MELODY**.)*

Did you love me?

MELODY. *Yes.* So much.

CRAIG. You promise?

*(**MELODY** nods. **CRAIG** smiles, satisfied.)*

We loved each other.

MELODY. We really did.

I didn't recognize it.

It would've gotten better, I would've gotten better I just –

CRAIG. I know. Me too.

MELODY. Are you going to go back to sleep?

CRAIG. Yes.

MELODY. Are you going to heaven?

> (**CRAIG** *nods.*)

> Have you seen it?

CRAIG. Yep! But only from far away.

MELODY. What's it like?

CRAIG. There's a house. Like ours.

MELODY. Do you have a bed?

CRAIG. Yes.

MELODY. Is it a twin or a full?

CRAIG. Full.

MELODY. Is there room for me in it?

> (**CRAIG** *doesn't respond.*)

> Is there?

CRAIG. We'll see.

> G'night Mel.

MELODY. G'night –

CRAIG. I love you.

> Oh, it's Craig.

> (**MELODY** *smiles, laughs.*)

> (**CRAIG** *kisses her forehead.* **MELODY** *nods.*)

MELODY. Sleep tight.

> (*Slowly,* **CRAIG** *goes.* **MELODY** *watches in silence.*)

> (*Dark.*)

The End

Also by
Bekah Brunstetter...

F*cking Art

I Used to Write on Walls

OOHRAH!

Sick

OTHER TITLES AVAILABLE FROM SAMUEL FRENCH

OOHRAH!

Bekah Brunstetter

Dramatic Comedy / 4m, 3f / Interior Set

Ron is back from his third and final tour in Iraq, and his wife Sara is excited to restart their life together in their new home. When a young marine visits the family, life is turned upside down. Sara's sister is swept off her feet; her daughter Lacey trades her dresses for combat boots, and Ron gets hungry for real military action. In this disarmingly funny and candid drama, Bekah Brunstetter raises challenging questions about what it means when the military is woven into the fabric of a family, and service is far more than just a job.

"The young scribe's talent and potential are obvious in this Southern-basted dramatic comedy about the war mystique as it plays out on the American home front…"
— *Variety*

"…Poignancy and terrific humor in both the writing and performances…"
— *Theatremania.com*

"If there's anything that stands out about Oohrah! at the Atlantic Theater Company's Stage II, it's the off-Broadway introduction of playwright Bekah Brunstetter, whose play is a fascinating, original take on something we've come to see rather often nowadays: the war play…. Let's hope we hear her voice uptown again real soon."
— *NYTheatre.com*

"The play skillfully depicts how the demands of military service affect an individual family and society as a whole. Brunstetter's people are real and funny. She never condescends to them or treats them as symbols to put a point across…A big hurrah for *Oohrah!*"
— *Backstage*

OTHER TITLES AVAILABLE FROM SAMUEL FRENCH

I USED TO WRITE ON WALLS

Bekah Brunstetter

Drama / 1m, 6f / Unit Set

Diane, Georgia and Joanne are 3 modern women living very different lives. Unbeknownst to them, they are all pining after the same young man, Trevor: sexy, stoned, oblivious; a surfer on a rad, rad philosophical journey. When a beautiful 11 year old girl named Anna, and Mona (a sexy, widowed astronaut) are thrown into the crosswinds of diverse romantic affairs, hearts will be broken, loves will be lost, and youthful cries of hope, anger, and sadness will be written on walls. Mothers will try to guide their daughters from the promise and beauty of youth through the diminishing opportunities of aging. Daughters will go to the extremes of passion to hold on to their fantasies of love. One man will be in the middle of a romantic storm of graffiti, drugs, sexual asphyxiation, gunshots, explosions, and desire.